D1559783

21st-Century Education and Careers

Options and Strategies

A YOUNG MAN'S GUIDE
TO CONTEMPORARY ISSUES™

21st-Century Education and Careers

Options and Strategies

Molly Jones

New York

Published in 2012 by The Rosen Publishing Group, Inc.
29 East 21st Street, New York, NY 10010

Library of Congress Cataloging-in-Publication Data

Jones, Molly, 1933–
21st-century education and careers: options and strategies/
Molly Jones. — 1st ed.
    p. cm. — (A young man's guide to contemporary issues)
Includes bibliographical references and index.
ISBN 978-1-4488-5526-1 (library binding)
1. High school student orientation — United States — Juvenile
literature. 2. High school boys — Vocational guidance — United
States — Juvenile literature. 3. Boys-Education (Secondary) —
United States — Juvenile literature. 4. College student
orientation — United States — Juvenile literature. I. Title.
LB1620.6.J66 2012
378.1'980973 — dc23
                                                        2011018746

Manufactured in the United States of America

CPSIA Compliance Information: Batch #W12YA: For further information, contact Rosen Publishing, New York, New
York, at 1-800-237-9932.

Contents

INTRODUCTION

Young men have always faced obstacles and pitfalls when navigating high school. Dealing with the everyday demands and expectations of school is tough enough. But high school is also a time when you are feeling the pressures of what lies beyond—the world of colleges and careers. It can be hard to imagine your life ahead, much less figure out what you should be doing about it.

Despite progress in technology, some developments in the twenty-first century appear to be making life more challenging, rather than easier. The good news is, you can set goals for high school and beyond and build a strategy to reach them. The key is being proactive and taking charge of your own life.

You are launching your life at an exciting time. Your generation will explore and acquire new understandings in biology, neurology, quantum physics, chemistry, astronomy, and earth science. You will make use of many new discoveries, not only on and within Earth and its submicroscopic components, but also far beyond to the mind-stretching expanses of the known universe. Growing knowledge of psychology and the brain may assist you in harnessing the power of your personal traits, habits, choices, and actions, and help steer you toward your goals.

In the twenty-first century, your century, the world itself and individual lives within it will change at speeds and in directions we cannot now imagine. Though you can't foresee what these changes will be, you can prepare yourself for them. You can acquire the tools and skills to deal effectively with change, and you can plan ahead to make choices that will open doors for you instead of closing them.

CHAPTER 1

CHALLENGE, CHANGE, AND CAREERS

If we had to choose one word to describe today's world, that word might be "change." As a boy today, you and every corner of your life will be affected by change. From food to entertainment, from cancer treatment to gene therapy, from the accelerating speed of communication to growing threats to your privacy, nothing will be left untouched.

New scientific knowledge pours in minute by minute, and technology constantly changes. Every day when you wake up, the world around you will be significantly different from the day before. The next computer you buy will store many times more data in far smaller spaces than your present computer. People, as well as products, will move with never-before-imagined speeds across the country and around the globe.

How can you learn all you need to know to navigate high school successfully, prepare for college, and think

Technology skills are essential for nearly all academic and career pursuits today. Well-prepared students learn to use computers to conduct research, record and analyze data, and prepare reports.

about a career? Along with other global changes, careers, too, will change. To meet this challenge, education will change, and you will be a part of this exciting and dynamic world.

The Explosion of Information and Knowledge

While acceleration in digital speed and power is central to recent global changes, it is not the whole story. In fact, the explosion of information in recent decades might well be called the "big bang" of the twenty-first century. Knowledge today dwarfs the knowledge that your father or even your older brother could have imagined.

Robert Brown, dean of continual education at the University of North Carolina–Greensboro, spoke to his students about the sheer volume of knowledge now available to everyone. While knowledge doubled in the three hundred years between 1450 and 1750, Brown estimated that medical knowledge now doubles every seven years. Today, the total of human knowledge is believed to double every two to three years, and by

2020, some expect knowledge to double every seventy-two days.

Alongside this tidal wave of knowledge, the barrage of media increases and changes every day. Music, videos, games, applications, and Web sites proliferate by the millions. Social networking sites and text messaging provide a nonstop flow of images and messages from friends and strangers alike who want your attention, your time, and sometimes your money.

For about two hundred thousand years, the humans that existed were physically like today's humans, according to an article by Hillary Mayell in *National Geographic News*. For the last fifty thousand of those years, humans have had language, thought processes, and cultural patterns much like ours. Over most of that time, change occurred slowly.

Now, in only the last few decades, electronics and media have upended daily life, including school life, in a way and at a speed that no one has experienced before. While human physical and mental characteristics haven't changed significantly for fifty thousand years, the world is very different from the one humans lived in fifty thousand years ago, and it will become even more different tomorrow and every year.

No one knows how the accelerating flood of media, messages, information, and technological change will affect people's minds and bodies over time. As neuroscientist Francis Jenson of Children's Hospital Boston noted, human brains have never before experienced a nonstop tidal wave of information like the one we have today.

Because of rapid and constant change and the explosion of knowledge, schools will be challenged in teaching the necessary skills. Learning through self-study, team projects, and the Web will require being self-directed and self-motivated. Students will need to learn to focus in the midst of disruption, find and organize resources and information, and manage time with minimal supervision.

Learning in a Changing World

In addition to technological change and the explosion of knowledge, the world is evolving in ways that will strongly affect education and preparation for a career. The globalization that is taking place in almost every area of life, as well as the snowballing damage and threat to the natural environment, are changing life at a rapid pace. How do these changes affect you, the education you will need, and your career options?

First, increased globalization in nearly every field changes what students need to know and how they will learn it. Although you still need to understand your local community and country, what you see, hear, and learn will increasingly focus on the entire globe as your community. Whether in manufacturing, banking, space travel, food production and distribution, water resources, transportation, health, environmental protection, or technology, action taken in one part of the world increasingly affects every other part of the world.

You will live in an accelerating digital world in which you will be working alongside people of other nationalities

on projects or problems that are world concerns. A cattle
disease in Wisconsin, an extended hard freeze in Florida,
or a ban on whaling in the northern Atlantic affects the
global food supply. War in the Middle East affects the
world energy supply. Factory smoke in China affects

Environmental advocates celebrate the fortieth anniversary of Earth Day in Washington, D.C., with a skit about global warming. Many twenty-first century students will train for careers solving environmental problems.

global air quality. A human disease that develops in Africa may spread and cause millions of deaths. An oil spill in any ocean will affect all parts of the world.

The ways in which the environment has been abused and natural resources depleted are themselves global

JOIN THE WORLD! FIVE SMART REASONS TO LEARN A SECOND (OR THIRD!) LANGUAGE

There are a number of reasons why young people today should learn a language (or languages) in addition to English:

- According to the American Council on the Teaching of Foreign Languages (ACTFL), studies have shown that students who study a foreign language score higher on the SAT and ACT exams.
- Studying foreign languages improves chances of entry into college and graduate schools.
- Knowing additional languages can open up many job and business opportunities.
- Multilingual candidates will likely qualify for jobs with higher pay.
- In a time of rapid globalization, you will be better able to understand and deal with diverse cultural ideas, live alongside people with diverse lifestyles, and communicate with those from different cultures.

problems. As the natural environment changes rapidly, many skilled leaders and workers with a wide range of knowledge will be needed. Experts in science, engineering, farming, sanitation, wildlife protection, forestry, water resources, transportation, energy, psychology, management, and other fields will be needed during your adult life to stabilize and maintain a livable environment around the globe.

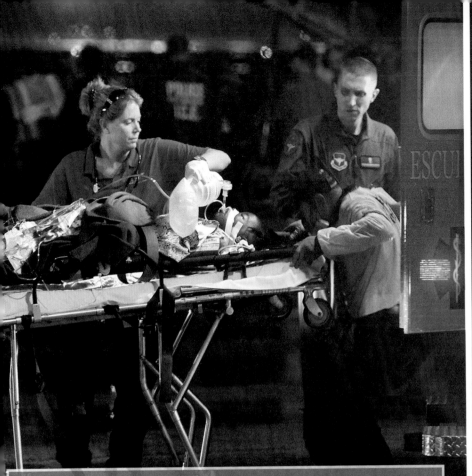

Many students pursue careers that enable them to save lives and relieve suffering. Here, paramedics in West Palm Beach, Florida, transport a person injured in the massive 2010 earthquake in Haiti.

Many careers will likely be reshaped in order to take into account multilingual and multicultural employees and operations. Understanding our global interdependence, being open to working with others who may think differently from you, and practicing skills of cooperation and problem solving both in school and outside will be important steps in preparation for your future.

A World of Human Need

Many factors in modern life have widened the gap between those who have the resources to live comfortably and those whose circumstances deny them even the bare necessities. Loss of water resources, deforestation, pollution, diseases such as HIV/AIDS and tuberculosis, war, and natural disasters are among the causes of human misery and an increase in poverty.

Our changing environment, globalization, and humanitarian needs suggest many interesting and rewarding career possibilities. But whatever you choose to study, learning more about environmental change, globalization, and ways of preventing or reversing human suffering will put you a step ahead.

CHAPTER 2

WHAT CHALLENGES ARE YOUNG MEN FACING?

Not only is the world around you changing, but even what you are expected to be and do as a young man has changed and will continue to change. Job opportunities available to young men in the economy are in flux.

In addition, while some boys are succeeding in school, others are facing academic challenges. Some of these challenges include learning disabilities and attention-deficit/hyperactivity disorder (ADHD); low grades and standardized test scores; disciplinary problems; and lower rates of high school and college completion than girls. The good news is, with strong goals for the future and support from adults in the community, many of these challenges can be overcome.

The Changing Role of Boys and Men

For centuries, the kinds of work that men and women did were seldom the same. For much of Western history, men

entered trades and professions, while women did "woman's work" inside the home. When they did work in similar jobs, men's wages were higher than women's. During the twentieth century, American women fought for equality with men, including the right to be employed at the same jobs as men and be paid equally for doing identical work.

In the twenty-first century, both boys and girls often train for careers formerly dominated by men. Here, hearing-impaired high school students in Austin, Texas, learn to repair computers.

As a result, young women graduating from high school and college now apply to study for the same career fields that were once limited to males. For example, young men now compete not only with other young men but also with competent young women for admission to colleges and professional schools. Until the late 1970s, the number of men earning college and graduate degrees greatly exceeded the number of degree-earning women. Today, men are the minority in college enrollment, and according to the 2009 Shriver Report, women earn 60 percent of the college degrees awarded each year. Not only in colleges, but also in graduate schools of medicine, law, veterinary medicine, and many other fields, the number of women often matches or exceeds the number of men. On the job as well, men now compete with women for assignments and promotions and for political offices.

Economic forces have also changed the landscape for men at work. In recent years, manufacturing—a traditional area of employment for men without a college degree— has lost many jobs due to automation (machines replacing human labor), increases in productivity, and international competition. At the same time, the service sector of the American economy, in which men are the minority, has expanded. According to the U.S. Bureau of Labor Statistics (BLS), these trends are expected to continue through 2018.

Just as in the workplace, the roles of men and women in families have changed. More men are choosing to be active caregivers to their children, take family leave when their children are born, work at home, and help care for elderly or disabled family members. Sometimes, when both spouses work, a wife may earn more than her husband. At other times, women may be the breadwinners while men help with child care and household duties. Either may happen by mutual choice or because of job loss. For many families today, the man as the main breadwinner and "head of the household" is an idea that is no longer useful or fair.

Is There a "Boy Crisis"?

In recent years, leaders in education have become concerned about the state of boys in school. Statistics suggest that boys aren't learning as well as girls in many areas and that they are facing many challenges. A fact sheet from the U.S. Department of Health and Human Services (HHS) gives the following statistics:

- Boys are almost three times as likely as girls to be diagnosed with ADHD — 11 percent vs. 4 percent.

- Boys are almost twice as likely as girls to be diagnosed with a learning disability — 10 percent vs. 6 percent.

- More than two-thirds of all students who receive special education services are male.

- Boys have higher rates of suspensions and expulsions than girls, regardless of race or ethnicity.

- Boys drop out of high school at a higher rate than girls.

The problem of school dropouts is perhaps the most alarming. According to *Diplomas Count 2010*, a special publication from *Education Week*, only about two-thirds (or 66 percent) of male students in the United States today earn

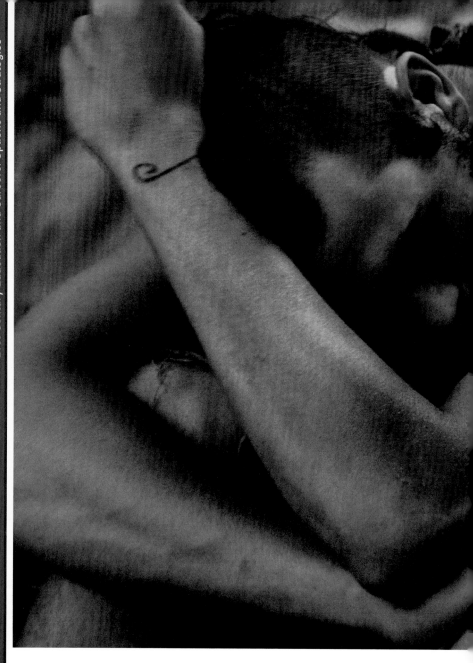

a high school diploma. This graduation rate is 7 percentage points lower than the rate for female students. Rates of high school completion for boys from minority groups, such as Latinos, African Americans, and Native Americans, are even lower—hovering around the 50 percent mark.

A student rests during an activity at the Center for Attention and Related Disorders camp in Connecticut. ADHD, which affects more boys than girls, is an obstacle in some boys' academic achievement.

Unfortunately, dropping out of high school is very costly to individual boys and to society. According to the HHS, boys without a high school diploma experience higher unemployment and are at greater risk for problems such as poverty and criminal activity.

STATISTICS ON TEEN BOYS AND HIGH-RISK OR FATAL BEHAVIORS

- According to a report from the Office of Juvenile Justice and Delinquency Prevention (OJJDP), 71 percent of teens arrested for aggravated assault in 2005 were boys.
- According to the 2005 CDC Youth Risk Surveillance, a report from the Centers for Disease Control and Prevention (CDC), 29.8 percent of boys and 7.1 percent of girls reported carrying a weapon in the past month.
- According to a 2009 story by National Public Radio (NPR), 75 percent of the six thousand teen drivers involved in fatal car crashes in 2008 were boys.
- According to 2009 data from the CDC, 84 percent of the young adults who die from suicide are male.

While experts agree that boys seem to be underachieving in school, there are many different views about why this is happening, and there seem to be no easy answers. Some educators are exploring the idea that K–12 classrooms and curricula are not set up in boy-friendly ways. They are experimenting with new educational approaches that allow boys to do more physical movement in the classroom and engage in more hands-on learning. They are also developing programs that involve more competition, games, and teamwork. Education leaders hope these new approaches will make boys feel more comfortable in school and prevent them from developing negative attitudes toward school at a young age.

The High Price of Being Cool

Other experts believe that some boys have difficulty in school because of the social pressure that they face to be masculine. In his family, neighborhood, and school, a guy learns very early on that in order to be masculine, he must be tough. He learns from experience that boys don't cry; they never back down from a fight, no matter how unfair and unnecessary; and they never back down from a dare, however meaningless and harmful it might be.

Michael Thompson, co-author of the book *Raising Cain* and host of a PBS documentary of the same title, says boys believe that their road to manhood involves passing a series of tests. These physical and psychological tests differ from community to community. On PBS's Web site, Thompson states, "All the tests have common themes: strength, stoicism, and avoiding everything feminine. In rural Texas or New Hampshire, the test might be learning to hunt and kill a deer. For teens in a suburban town, it might be doing something illegal: driving without a license or drinking. For many boys who want to be cool, it may mean not doing well in school."

Boys sometimes pay a painful price when they believe that they must conform to the expectations of other students. Thinking they must be cool and tough and pass certain tests in order to survive, they sometimes fail to make the kinds of choices that would lead to academic success. Some fall behind in classes and get into trouble. Others drop out of school, abuse alcohol or illegal drugs, become addicted to tobacco, and cause serious or even fatal car

accidents. Some boys on this negative road become depressed or even commit suicide.

What if you were one of these statistics? It would be easy to blame your actions on peer pressure, the failings of

Use of illegal drugs and alcohol is associated with many negative consequences, including poor performance in school, accidents, violence, and suicide.

your parents, or the fact that you were born a guy. The fact is, though, your situation has a great deal to do with the choices that you make. The biggest question that you face in navigating school and preparing for the real world may

A young man in Colorado is arrested for stealing marijuana. According to the National Center for Juvenile Justice, arrest rates are higher for young males for all offenses except running away from home.

be, who will really be in charge of your life? Don't allow your desire to create a certain image get in the way of being who you really are and preparing for a solid future in school and a career. Making your own choices and taking responsibility for your own actions can help keep your life on a positive track.

The good news is, in preparing to thrive in this changing world, young men like you can seek new skills and explore options for adapting in positive ways. The coming chapters will explore ways that you can start confidently on the path to success.

CHAPTER 3

FINDING THE ROAD TO SCHOOL AND CAREER SUCCESS

Success doesn't mean the same thing to everyone. If you aspire to be a computer engineer and your friend Sam aspires to play violin with the New York Philharmonic, the two of you will take very different paths to success. In another sense, though, success has the same meaning for both of you. Success is arriving at the destination that you set out to reach. Though the specific knowledge and technical skills that you and Sam need are different, the same basic skills, personal traits, and habits will help each of you build a solid foundation.

Begin Your College and Career Planning with the Basics

It's not possible for you to learn now all the facts and mountains of information you will need to excel in science, environmental studies, electronics, medicine, or any other field. But you can master basic skills in math and language, as well as learn the techniques for obtaining the knowledge and information that you need.

THE KING OF BASICS

The most essential skills are reading and writing. Dr. Robert Pitcher of the University of Alabama Educational Development Center has cited poor language skills as a major factor contributing to student failure in college. A student's ability to read, write, speak, and listen effectively is often a determining element in college success.

On the job, too, strong language and communication skills are in high demand and necessary for success. According to a 2007 article by Lynn Olson in *Education Week*, employers want their workers to have better language skills than many high school graduates now possess.

A 2006 survey by the Conference Board, a business research organization, found that 72 percent of human resource managers rated new employees with a high school diploma as deficient in basic writing skills, such as grammar and spelling. Eighty-one percent rated these new hires as deficient in creating well-written documents, such as memos, letters, and reports. According to the organization Achieve, the ability to work in teams and orally present one's work is considered critical by employers as well.

Clearly, polishing one's language and communication skills will put a young employee or college student a step ahead. While in high school, become an avid reader and

To prepare yourself for the reading you will encounter in college and on the job, read as much as you can while you are still in high school.

regular writer. If this is difficult for you, talk to your language arts teacher or guidance counselor about getting extra help or coaching, or taking classes that focus on these skills.

Understanding the information and ideas you read, along with the ability to express facts and ideas in writing and orally, are necessary not only for success in college or a career but also in other high school courses. Read to know, read to succeed, and read for fun. Also write frequently, whether for an assignment, a school newspaper article, or a personal journal or blog. Readers and writers can learn and succeed at whatever they choose.

NEXT, DO THE NUMBERS

Confidence and ability in basic math skills are essential for a number of reasons. First, math basics are needed every day in almost every field. According to Achieve, mathematical reasoning, problem solving, and the ability to apply math to different tasks are the most important skills cited by college professors and employers.

In her article in *Education Week*, Olson interviewed Daniel Furman of the Fund for Colorado's Future. Furman had recently met a representative of the Denver pipe fitter's union. The representative was having trouble finding qualified employees. "He had just looked at one hundred applications," Furman said, "and he mentioned they just had weak math and science skills. For a pipe fitter, perhaps you don't assume that you need individuals with strong math and science skills, but in fact you really do."

In addition, lack of competence at math will close many doors in your future. At this time, you may not be interested in further math studies or in a science, engineering, or technical field, but your interests may change with

Even though calculators can perform math operations, being competent in basic math skills and concepts is essential for a student to understand the operations and apply them correctly.

experience. As you learn more about these fields and begin to feel more competent in them, they may become your top interests. Remember to do your research: the minimum number of math courses your high school requires for graduation may not be adequate for the college or tech program that you want to attend.

Finally, even if you don't plan a career in science or technology, mastery of basic math topics and processes will help you understand many other things in the world around you.

If you have already fallen behind in either language or math skills, talk to your guidance counselor or a favorite teacher about opportunities for extra help or coaching to bring you at least to your grade level in those subjects. Acting now to reinforce your foundation in the basics, either through self-study or extra help, will pave the road to the future that you want.

The Traits and Habits of Success

Psychologists have found that developing certain traits, habits, and skills can greatly increase a student's chance of achieving the goals he or she sets out to reach, whether in high school, college, or in the working world. These qualities include demonstrating personal responsibility, having a strong work ethic, being on time, and displaying a positive attitude.

Employers have also cited these skills—sometimes known as "soft" or "applied" skills—as critically important in the workplace. The nonprofit organization Partnership for 21st Century Skills has determined that "life and career skills," such as initiative and self-direction, are among the essential skills needed in the future. The following sections describe some specific traits and skills that can help you get ahead in school and in life.

Be the Captain of Your Own Ship

Successful students are self-determining and self-motivated. No one else decides what direction their ship will sail—they do. Rather than conform to peer pressure from other students, they think for themselves and set their own standards.

Being self-directed and self-motivated doesn't mean being unfriendly or not being a fun part of the crowd. It means sticking to your own principles, pursuing your own goals, and making your own choices. You can make choices that are in your own best interest in a friendly way, maybe even a humorous way, without criticizing the choices of others.

In addition, successful students and workers are self-starters. Rather than wait for a teacher, parent, or employer to tell them what to do, they think ahead and take the initiative to do what needs to be done.

It is also important to be goal-oriented and purposeful. Whether he uses a plan, a map, or a sailing chart, a ship's captain needs to decide where he wants to end up before calculating how to get there. Sailing successfully through high school is like that, too. Your goals are the channel markers that can keep you on course.

While working to reach your goals, having a vision of the skills and competencies you want to develop is important. Football coaches call it "skull practice." They often have their players mentally rehearse the plays and strategies that they will use in the game. Research has shown that picturing yourself successfully carrying out a skill can

improve your actual performance. Make a habit of picturing your academic goals, determining what actions are needed to get there, and seeing yourself taking those actions. Just as on the football field, your skull practice could have a strong, positive effect on what happens in your school life.

Whether in sports, academics, or personal skills, planning to succeed, expecting to succeed, and visualizing yourself succeeding will increase the actual likelihood of success.

PUT THE PRINCIPLE OF CAUSE AND EFFECT TO WORK FOR YOU

The cause-and-effect principle tells us that each choice we make and each action we take right now will have consequences in the future. The principle reminds us, too, that our present circumstances come about partly as a result of choices we made and actions we took in the past.

Cause and effect doesn't have favorites—it treats everyone the same. For example, if you (1) do your assignments every day and never get behind in your courses, (2) make a habit of going for extra help right away when you don't understand something in class, and (3) learn, practice, and use research skills to find out more about the topics and skills that you are studying, chances are higher that you will succeed in that course. But what do you think will happen if you decide not to be bothered with doing the assignments, going for help, or doing research on your own?

A 2006 study from Mathematica Policy Research suggested that people who believe success comes from hard work rather than luck (in other words, those who believe they must take consistent action in order to create their own success) show higher earnings and greater career success over the long term. In fact, an improvement in this personal trait was shown to be as important for some students as gains in academic scores.

The value of this attitude is that it inspires you to take active steps toward your goals. This, in turn, increases the likelihood that the results you want to happen will happen. There is no guarantee, of course, that the results will always be exactly what you intend. Factors such as natural disasters, economic changes, illnesses, accidents, and lack of information can cause your plans to go off track. But the likelihood that you will get where you want to go will soar once you make the power of cause and effect work for you instead of against you.

The difficult part is, understanding how cause and effect works means that we can no longer blame others when our choices cause us problems. Each of us must accept responsibility for our own choices and for our part in the actions of a larger group. When things go wrong, we can deny our mistakes and blame someone else, or we can study what happened, learn from the results, and take a different path next time.

RESPECT RULES AND LAWS, AND CONTRIBUTE TO THE COMMUNITY

In the United States, elected representatives make the rules and laws. People across the country have different opinions, experiences, and knowledge, so not everyone will agree with any particular rule or law. But a society in which people decide for themselves whether or not to stop at a stoplight or pay taxes would cause problems for everyone.

Most laws or rules either restrict what a person or group can do, or declare what they must do. A restrictive law is made to prevent a serious harm, make the community safer, or make it more enjoyable for most people. Examples of restrictive laws are speed limits and rules against carrying weapons, assaulting another person, building fires in a protected area, or possessing narcotics.

In schools, most rules and regulations are made by school officials, who are responsible for student safety, protection of school property, and creating an orderly place where students are able to learn. Sometimes, student

Build positive relationships with school staff. An admired teacher, administrator, or counselor can provide strong support and resources to help a student set and reach his school and career goals.

representatives have a role in setting the rules. For example, in some schools, the student council makes rules regarding student activities and organizations.

In schools, restrictive rules may prohibit hanging out in the hallway while classes are in session, smoking in restricted areas, bringing a weapon to school, or cheating on an exam. Mandatory school rules state what students are required to do, such as attend a certain number of days of class or earn four units in English to graduate.

People think about rules and laws in different ways. Some decide that breaking the law is a problem only if they get caught. Others believe that the law should apply only to people who aren't as smart, careful, or superior as they believe they are. A recent example of this is the story of Bernard Madoff, who ran a multibillion-dollar investment business. His business turned out to be a fraud, and its collapse wiped out the savings of thousands of investors and ruined charities. He is now serving a 150-year sentence in prison.

Students in school may think that way also. They may believe that smoking, keeping a knife in a locker, and cheating are mistakes only if you get caught. Also, students and adults alike may defy rules or laws because they feel unaccepted in the group.

According to Harvard psychologist Howard Gardner, too many young people and adults are prioritizing their own needs—including getting ahead and beating the competition—over doing the right thing. In his book *Five Minds for the Future*, Gardner argues that to prepare for success in the twenty-first century—and to make the world

STEPS TO SUCCESS IN HIGH SCHOOL AND BEYOND

- Stay in charge of your own life.
- Be goal-oriented and purposeful.
- Be flexible to adapt and grow in a changing world.
- Apply the principle of cause and effect to reach your goals.
- Take responsibility for your own choices and actions.
- Fulfill your responsibilities as a good citizen, and work for the good of the community.

the kind of place we want to live in—students need to develop what he calls "the ethical mind." In other words, people need to go beyond self-interest and consider the impact of their actions on the wider community. People must think about more than simply what they need to do to follow the law, but also what they can do to fulfill their responsibilities to others and make the world a better place.

Role Models for Success

It can help to be inspired by the stories of real men who have practiced the habits of success in their own lives. To find examples of role models, we can look to great achievers in history, present-day individuals who have overcome the odds, and even everyday people we know in the community.

A HISTORICAL EXAMPLE

More than a half century ago, the world watched, spell-bound, as the first astronauts from Russia and the United States showed the kind of toughness and determination that it takes to be well-prepared achievers.

In 1957, the United States was hard at work on what the nation believed was the world's leading space program. Space scientists thought they would soon launch the world's first satellite into space.

Suddenly, news came that the Soviet Union had successfully launched a satellite named *Sputnik* into space. American scientists and political leaders were stunned that another nation could be ahead of the United States in science and technology. Four years later, the American public was outraged when a Russian astronaut, Yuri Gagarin, became the first human to be launched into space.

Gagarin's thoughts about his achievement were not about popularity or acclaim. Following his flight into space, he said, "When I orbited the earth in a spaceship, I saw for the first time how beautiful our planet is. Mankind, let us preserve and increase this beauty, and not destroy it."

When Neil Armstrong stepped on the moon in 1969, America took the lead in the space race. Like Gagarin, Armstrong did not think about himself when reflecting on this achievement. After being honored as the first human to step on the moon, he said, "I wasn't chosen to be first. I was just chosen to command that flight. Circumstance put me in that particular role."

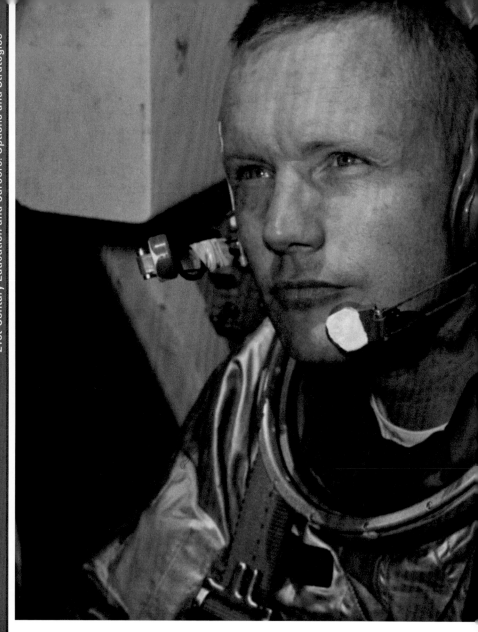

As high school students, neither Armstrong nor Gagarin expected to become an astronaut. Growing up, Armstrong was fascinated with flight, and by sixteen, he had earned his student pilot's license. His high school record earned him a U.S. Navy scholarship to Purdue University in West

From boyhood, Neil Armstrong, the first human to walk on the moon, persistently worked to achieve his life goals. In this 1965 photo, Armstrong is training for a Project Gemini space mission.

Lafayette, Indiana, where he earned a degree in aeronautical engineering. Later, he earned a master of science degree in aerospace engineering.

Gagarin also pursued his own goals in his secondary school years. He studied physics and mathematics and was an avid reader. He, too, had a strong interest in flight. While studying in a technical school, he joined a flying club and took his first solo flight in 1955.

By their own initiative and persistence, both Armstrong and Gagarin chose to pursue their own dreams and become competent and confident in their own areas of interest. Because of their self-determination and initiative, they were prepared to take advantage of opportunities when they came their way.

A Modern-Day Pact

Dr. Sampson Davis, Dr. Rameck Hunt, and Dr. George Jenkins grew up on the tough streets of Newark, New Jersey, one of the poorest cities in the country. Growing up surrounded by broken families, drugs, and crime, the three could have easily followed many of their peers into drug dealing, gangs, and prison. However, when the boys met as teenagers at University High School, a magnet school, they bonded. They agreed that they wanted to beat the odds and make more of their lives than what was expected of them.

The friends attended an information session about a special program at Seton Hall University that was designed to encourage minority students to pursue medical careers. After that, they made a pact: no matter what, they would stick together, graduate from college, and become doctors. Although they faced setbacks along the way, the three young men worked hard, separated themselves from negative influences, and sought out mentors. They never

Myths and Facts

Myth

Formal education beyond high school is not necessary for success.

Fact

While not every young man needs a four-year degree, some amount of higher education will be critical for success in the twenty-first century. According to a report from the Center on Education and the Workforce at Georgetown University, the share of U.S. jobs that required education beyond high school increased from 28 percent in 1973 to 59 percent in 2008. This share is expected to increase to 63 percent over the next decade. The report projects that by 2018, nine out of ten workers with a high school education or less will be concentrated in fields with low wages or that are in decline, such as food and personal services, sales and office support, and manual labor and manufacturing. On the other hand, workers with credentials beyond high school (vocational certificates, associate's degrees, and bachelor's degrees) will be in demand.

Myth

If you are not feeling engaged or excited by your high school education, there is nothing you can do about it. The only choices are to suffer through it or drop out.

Myths and Facts (continued)

Fact

Every high school student should be spending at least part of the day excited and energized by learning. Many high schools offer electives and other opportunities that can help you explore your interests. For example, taking a few courses in career and technical education can allow you to work hands-on and learn real-world skills. As long as you continue to fulfill the academic requirements for college, taking these classes doesn't have to mean that you are leaving the college track. Also, some high schools now allow students to spend part of the day attending a community college, doing a career internship, or working on an independent study course. Speak with a guidance counselor about how you can pursue your areas of interest.

Myth

The friends you choose to spend time with have no effect on whether or not you succeed in education or a career.

Fact

According to the HHS, having friends who are disruptive or who drop out of school can increase a student's risk for academic failure. However, involvement with positive peer activities and having good relationships with peers contributes to academic achievement.

allowed circumstances or peer pressure to determine what kind of students they would be.

Today, Hunt is an internist and assistant professor of medicine, Davis is an emergency medicine physician, and Jenkins serves as an assistant professor of clinical dentistry. The three tell the story of how they overcame obstacles and achieved their goals in the book *The Pact: Three Young Men Make a Promise and Fulfill a Dream.*

On the three doctors' Web site, Davis states, "Strength comes from knowing that the power to overcome adversity and prevail lies within one's self and you have to first realize that. Once realized, you have to accept account-ability for your life and take the necessary steps to turn hopes and dreams into realities."

CHAPTER 4

PREPARING FOR LIFE AFTER HIGH SCHOOL

The road from high school to a career is one of the most exciting paths you will ever travel. High school is for living life here and now, exploring new ideas, developing extra-curricular interests, and laying a solid academic foundation. It is also a time to begin discovering your real values and priorities, and thinking about the direction your adult life will take. During this period, you are preparing for further studies in college, technical school, or on-the-job training—and thinking about a career. But what studies, and what career?

Many students graduate from academic or technical colleges still unsure of their career direction. However, thinking ahead about colleges and careers can help you make good decisions about courses and activities in both high school and college. This chapter will describe several processes you can pursue in high school to prepare you to make solid college and career decisions when the time comes.

Who Am I, Really?

According to the Center for Career Opportunities at Purdue University, getting to know yourself is the best way to start making choices about both college and career. Your own goals, passions, and aptitudes are your best clues to selecting high school courses, a college major, and your life's work. Learning what you do well and what you enjoy most will help you decide whether to pursue a creative talent, work to protect the environment, or launch a career in the business world.

Career counselors at Purdue suggest these questions to ask yourself as you explore post–high school options:

1. What are your dreams? If you could be anything you wanted to be, regardless of money or education, what would it be?
2. What are your main interests? If there were no requirements, what would you read, study, and learn about on your own? (You can also ask your guidance counselor to give you an interest inventory to help you identify your interests.)
3. What are your top abilities? What subjects do you make the best grades in? What achievements are you most proud of?
4. What are your values, that is, the things that are most important to you in life? If you had a million dollars with no strings attached, what would you do with it?
5. What have you learned about yourself from your life experiences? What have you liked and disliked about the activities, jobs, or volunteer experiences you've had?

Think about some success stories or achievements from your past, whether you were in school, participating in outside activities, or doing something on your own or for your family. What were you doing when you were happiest and most proud of yourself? Were you working alone or with others? Were you doing physical or mental activities? Were you working with the natural environment, such

A talented nineteen-year-old pianist plays keyboards during a recording session at Rhymes 4 Reasons, an after-school program in Newark, New Jersey. Participants learn about the music business and audio engineering.

as with plants or animals; with electronic equipment; with people who had special needs; or were you reading? Imagine a career in which you can do many of the kinds of activities you enjoy most.

In addition to doing a self-study of your interests, take an objective test such as an interest inventory or career aptitude test, which your guidance counselor can provide. Your guidance counselor can administer the tests to you, evaluate the results, and help you discover career interests that you may not have considered before. Taking these tests may help you get a better sense of your aptitudes—those areas in which you have the potential to do well. You may find that you have strong potential in areas you have not personally experienced and had not previously considered as possibilities.

Focusing In on Careers: Where Will You Fit?

Once you have a realistic image of your interests and strengths, you can start to use the Internet and the library to broaden your knowledge about the wide range of careers open to you. As you begin to research careers and colleges, start a loose-leaf notebook or series of computer files in which you can summarize the information you gather. Begin with a page for each career you look into, and then a page for each college you consider. You can add pages when needed.

Some that you might explore are environmental careers, computer science careers, and humanitarian careers, as well as careers in health care, business, education, engineering, technical fields, and many others.

Use this notebook or computer database throughout high school. When decision time for college or a career arrives, you will have a valuable resource for making wise choices.

An abundance of information about careers is available on the Internet, at the library, and from your connections with people in many fields. Use your Web browser to select several areas that fit your personality traits, aptitudes, and interests. For example, you can insert a phrase such as "careers in sports," "careers in graphic arts," "green careers," "careers in finance," or "careers in law enforcement." Also explore job categories such as "jobs requiring technical certification," "jobs for people with disabilities," "multilingual jobs," or other categories that might fit your interests.

As you research, select individual jobs that you find interesting and read about them. Does the job involve skills, areas of knowledge, and activities and tasks that you think you would enjoy? Also note what education level and other credentials are required. For example, you might search for "athletic trainer qualifications," "qualifications for a medical records technician," or "paralegal qualifications." Add any information that may be helpful in the future to your careers and colleges notebook. This information may be helpful when selecting your high school or college courses.

On sites that describe qualifications for a particular job, you may find a section describing the job outlook. This section explains whether more or fewer positions in that job category are expected in the coming years. Also, every two years, the U.S. Department of Labor publishes the *Occupational Outlook Handbook*, which describes and assesses the outlook for jobs in hundreds of career areas.

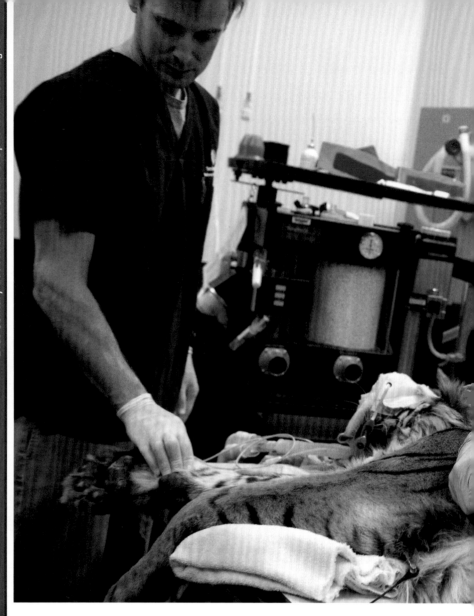

The handbook, available both in print and online, can help you determine if a job you are interested in is likely to be a good long-term career prospect.

It is also a good idea to talk to people who currently work in the field and get their honest opinions about the outlook for that career area. You can contact professionals

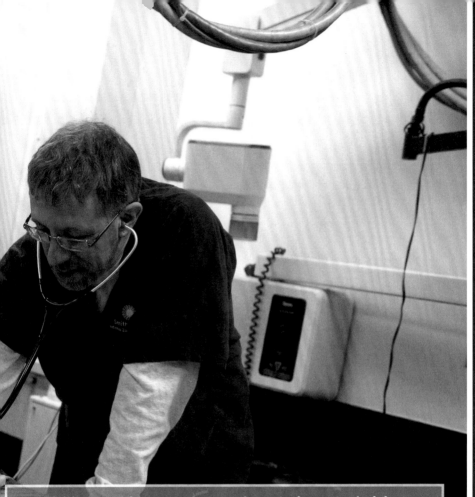

A visiting veterinary student and a veterinary technician examine Soy, a Sumatran tiger, at the National Zoo in Washington, D.C. Though admission to veterinary school is competitive, job prospects are good.

in the community for informational interviews, in which you ask questions to learn more about the field. One good question to ask is whether their field seems to be expanding or contracting in terms of career opportunities. A job's outlook is important to consider before investing years of time and money to become qualified in the area.

THE 10 FASTEST-GROWING JOBS AND THEIR PERCENT GROWTH BY 2016

According to data from the BLS, the following jobs are expected to be the fastest-growing careers through 2016:

Job	Percent Growth Expected
Network systems and data communications analyst	53.4 %
Personal and home care aide	50.6 %
Home health aide	48.7 %
Computer applications software engineer	44.6 %
Veterinary technologist and technician	41.0 %
Personal financial advisor	41.0 %
Theater and performance makeup artist	39.8 %
Medical assistant	35.4 %
Veterinarian	27.6 %
Substance abuse and behavioral disorders counselor	34.3 %

Because of rapid global, environmental, economic, and technological changes, some jobs you learn about now will have changed by the time you are ready to apply for a full-time job. New, well-paid jobs often require a higher level of education than those they replace. Thus, it's more important than ever to be competent in basic skills and prepared to pursue training at higher levels than what you may have expected initially.

Getting Acquainted with Colleges and Technical Schools

In addition to providing resources describing various careers, the Web is a great place to research post–high school education options. There are Web sites that list all of the major four-year academic colleges in the country or in your region, as well as all of the two-year or technical colleges where students can acquire specific job skills. These Web sites classify colleges in various ways and provide a wealth of information about them.

To begin selecting possibilities, first consider the maximum distance away your college can be. Estimate the tuition and living costs that you and your family can afford. Also, think about the size and type of school that you prefer, such as publicly supported or religiously affiliated.

Each year the magazine *U.S. News and World Report* lists the top colleges and universities across the country and by region in all major fields of study. In the special colleges issue, you can identify colleges within your distance, cost,

and type preferences. From this list, you can select the colleges whose specialties fit your career interests and aptitudes. You can then study the schools' individual Web sites in detail.

For many boys, the cost of college can be the main hurdle in reaching education and career goals. Though

Students in Los Angeles, California, attend a college and career convention in 2010, where they applied for jobs and student financial aid, and participated in college preparation workshops.

student loans are available, graduating with a large debt places a heavy burden on a young man or his family. Surprisingly, many available scholarships are left unclaimed each year because students don't apply for them. Links to scholarship information may be found on individual college Web sites. Your high school guidance counselor can also help you locate possible sources of scholarship funds. Be proactive in seeking scholarships to help you afford your college expenses.

If you are interested in technical education, you can collect information about potential schools in a similar way. Long before the time comes to actually apply to colleges or technical schools, write for, or download, an application from each institution you consider a possibility.

Studying Web sites and application materials gives you a good start at comparing colleges and considering how you would fit in at each school. Once you have narrowed your focus to a few colleges, begin to arrange visits to as many campuses as possible. Talk to students, visit classes, and talk with faculty members in your areas of interest. Just get a feel for what it is like to be there. While you are there, make an appointment with a staff member to learn about scholarships for which you might apply.

Then, in your junior or senior year, armed with a notebook or database full of information about careers and colleges, you can make some decisions.

College, Tech, or Work: What's Right for You?

Not every young man goes to college, and you may not know yet whether college is right for you. If you could know for sure in high school what your lifelong career would be, the answer might be easy: choose a college or technical school that is tops in that field. However, according to the Center for Career Opportunities at Purdue

University, many students aren't sure about their career even after being in college for a year or more. About half of all students change majors at least once before graduating, and some change several times. For this reason, a college's specialty is not the only thing to consider in deciding where you will study. A college's location, cost, and overall atmosphere are important, too.

Many fast-growing, rewarding careers do not require a four-year college degree. But many of those careers still require people who are highly trained in specific skills that involve education beyond high school. In the medical field, for example, some technical careers may not require a four-year degree. Skills for these careers may often be obtained at a one- or two-year technical college or through a two-year associate's program at a community college. These jobs include physical or occupational therapist assistants, veterinary technologists or technicians, fitness trainers, dental hygienists or assistants, respiratory therapists, and others. Tech colleges offer specific job training in many areas, such as auto mechanics, electronics, cosmetology, culinary arts, and computer support services.

Other careers require only a high school diploma or GED. New employees are trained on the job or sent by their employers to workshops or schools for training.

Looking into careers that require different levels of education may suggest interesting possibilities you hadn't considered before. Add those to your notebook, and use your computer browser and library to investigate them further. It is especially important to learn what people in

those career areas actually do, and visualize yourself doing those things. When you are seriously interested in a career area, create opportunities to volunteer, work part-time, or visit and shadow an employee in that field. "Shadowing" means following a person during the work-day and observing him or her in order to learn about the job's responsibilities.

While training for a career in the food industry, a student watches a chef fillet a fish at the California Culinary Academy in San Francisco.

Get a Head Start

Even though you are a full-time student, you can get a head start in your career by actually gaining some experience in your projected profession or career. For example, if you hope to have a writing career, be a writer now. Write for your school publications. Arrange to shadow and assist

FIVE WAYS TO "TRY ON" YOUR FUTURE

There are a number of ways to test whether a career might be right for you before committing to that path. The following are some ideas:

1. Arrange to visit someone who works in a field you are interested in. Observe what a day on the job is really like. Watch how the person deals with problems that come up.
2. Interview people in, or retired from, a career you are interested in.
3. Read biographies of people in a wide range of careers. Consider whether you would fit in each career field.
4. Ask to be a summer intern or a volunteer in a workplace related to your career interests.
5. Acquire a mentor whom you respect and admire. This is an experienced career person who agrees to share advice and coach you informally. The mentor can talk with you about your future and what careers might fit your abilities and interests.

a reporter on your local newspaper staff. Write and submit stories and articles to magazines that publish youth writings. Read books from your public library about the genres of writing you are especially interested in. Don't settle for being interested in writing—do the things a writer does.

The same is true of other career areas. During summer vacation, look for chances to intern or volunteer in a business or organization in one of your areas of interest. As well as gaining insights into what a career in that field might be like, taking this kind of initiative will be a big plus on your college or job applications. You can also make personal connections that may help you when it is time to look for a job.

Selling Yourself: Applications, Résumés, Transcripts, and Interviews

Joan Eison, whose firm, Reset3, specializes in personal and career coaching, advises students to think well in advance about applications they will someday make for colleges and jobs. She reminds people that when listing work experience in an application, many kinds of work may be relevant, whether or not the work was a paying job.

"Every bit of experience counts," Eison says.

Actual paying jobs you have held as a teenager can be included in an application. But skills are also acquired through volunteer jobs and the responsibilities you take on in organizations. Handling funds, performing secretarial duties, working in a political campaign, being manager or trainer of a school athletic team, volunteer tutoring of other students, writing for school publications, or managing a school radio station—all provide valuable skills and experience.

To boost your qualifications, be proactive. Eison advises that you seek out opportunities in your school and commu-nity to work at many kinds of jobs. You will acquire skills and experience, and you will learn about yourself and

what kinds of activities you like best. Employers and college admissions staff will be impressed with your energy and initiative, whether you work for pay or as a volunteer.

Once you have met the basic requirements for acceptance at a college or for a job, a personal interview is often required. From the feedback she has received from

In Oregon, a Native American teenage boy presents his résumé at a job interview. Showing interest and enthusiasm, along with sharing a well-prepared résumé, creates a positive impression.

interviewers, Eison has learned which student characteristics give a positive or negative impression.

"Tuck your shirttail in," she says. Arriving with a sloppy appearance shows disrespect for the interviewer and for the job or school. Arriving on time, speaking clearly, making eye contact, and showing enthusiasm for and knowledge about the school or job will get you off to a good start.

In short, when completing an application or résumé, or when heading to an interview, think like a college admissions board member or future employer. Taking the time to understand the organization's goals and needs will help your chances of becoming part of the student body or one of the company's employees.

Life Beyond Academics and Career

For all of your youth, you have been a boy in your parents' family. Before many more years, you may become a husband or a committed life companion, a responsible breadwinner and leader within your family, and even a father and loving role model for your own children.

Some schools do not have specific offerings to prepare you for these roles. However, if your school offers courses in psychology, family finances, or child care, these can be starters in thinking about adult responsibilities.

Another positive strategy is to observe the interactions and relationships within your current family, the families of friends and relatives, and families in books and stories. Make note of attitudes and behaviors that create strong ties and supportive relationships, as well as characteristics and behaviors that seem to strain or break down family trust and supportiveness. Mentally create the family you would like to build with your life partner, and remind yourself of the characteristics you hope to emulate in order to achieve such a family.

Ten Great Questions
TO ASK A COUNSELOR

1.
Do my grades and test scores indicate that I could do well in college?

2.
Am I working at my top ability? If not, what can I do to improve?

3.
What skills should all students learn, regardless of what career they will choose?

4.
How can I find out what kinds of work I would be best at doing?

5.
How can I find a mentor to help me make career and college decisions?

6.
Should I decide on a career first, or a college?

7.
How can I arrange to shadow someone in each career area that I am interested in?

8.
What is the best strategy to prepare for success on the SAT or ACT?

9.
How can I get the extra help I need when my family can't afford to pay a tutor?

10.
Where can I find information about college scholarships for which I might qualify?

CHAPTER 5

THE WORLD WIDE WEB AND YOU

Unlike your parents and grandparents, you and your friends have grown up with computer technology in schools and almost everywhere you go. You know how to e-mail, send texts, find information online, and have fun on the Internet with games, videos, music, and more. The Web keeps you informed about science developments, international events, natural disasters, sports, and politics. Besides keeping you in touch and informed, computer technology can support and contribute in many ways to your success both in school and in preparing for a career.

Staying in Charge

Vast numbers of Web sites exist to sell products. Many others, such as those operated by the government, newspapers, magazines, TV channels, and universities, exist to provide information. Others exist to express personal opinions or promote a belief, idea, or philosophy. As a student, your challenge is to choose among these millions of Web sites ones that offer safe, accurate, and useful information.

There are no controls on the accuracy or quality of what is posted on a Web site, except those controls that organizations or companies apply to their own sites. Typically, no outside person or group checks to see if claims are true or if academic facts or explanations are accurate. Many Internet service providers offer information about Web site content for parents or schools that may want to limit what children watch. Any individuals or groups, however, can create their own Web sites and post nearly anything they like.

Three major mistakes that many teenage boys make when using the Internet can later become major hurdles to their school success. In fact, these mistakes can follow people as they seek entrance to college or a career. They include (1) allowing the Internet to take control of their time, (2) failing to consider the consequences when they post personal information or thoughtless comments online, and (3) using unreliable Web sites when studying or completing writing assignments. Understanding these mistakes and thinking ahead about ways to avoid them can prevent many problems now and in the future.

Managing Your Time

When boys reach high school, many new and interesting opportunities suddenly open up, all demanding time and attention. School courses are harder and require more study time. Sports, music, and other extracurricular interests take time for practice and study. Some boys

take on an after-school or weekend job to earn spending money or help with family expenses. Staying in control of one's time and attention can have a big effect on school success.

When students manage their time well, the computer can be a valuable tool for achieving academic and career goals.

The computer and the Internet can help you succeed in school. But they can also rob you of time and steer you off course. The key is to stay in control of your time and attention when using the computer.

Web sites that offer entertainment, such as games, videos, and popular music, are usually closely linked to commercial Web sites, which offer goods or services for purchase. These sites are often designed to lead you to other entertainment and commercial sites. They also make it easy to switch accidentally to Web sites or advertisements that you didn't intend to visit.

Reaching your education and career goals requires being proactive, that is, staying in control and making choices that prevent problems down the road. When you use the Internet, think carefully about how you want to use your time, and what you will or won't become involved in.

Recent studies have investigated the amount of time that young people spend on the Internet and other media and how these activities affect their school success. In 2010, research from the Kaiser Family Foundation showed that boys ages eight to eighteen spend an average of ninety-seven minutes per day on the Internet doing things unrelated to schoolwork. Boys who play video games (on console players, handheld players, and phones) spend another ninety-seven minutes per day playing, a larger amount of time for boys than for girls. In addition, boys spend on average another four hours and forty minutes per day watching television content.

According to a 2009 article in the journal *Adolescence*, high school boys who use the Internet to supplement what they read and learn in their classes tend to get better grades. But boys who use the computer and Internet mostly to play online games get lower grades than those who seldom play online games.

According to expert Michael Gurian, boys may be drawn to video games because, compared to girls, boys have more brain areas dedicated to spatial-mechanical functioning.

The constant and simultaneous use of digital media and communication, such as game playing, movies, Web surfing, texting, and listening to music, often leads to what researchers have called "information overload" or "infomania." In this phenomenon, the brain is forced to process a volume of information that it is not equipped to handle all at once. A study carried out at the University of London in 2005 showed that unchecked infomania often resulted in a reduction of mental ability greater than that from sleep loss or marijuana use.

How can you stay in control of your time on the Internet? Try making a bargain with yourself. For example, set aside fifteen minutes after school to relax by playing

your favorite game. In return, agree that you will then go directly to your homework, using the computer only in ways that contribute to getting your work done or finding out more about the topics you are studying. Agree that you will stick with your schoolwork until it's done before you switch back to the Internet or any other activities.

Think Before You Post

Although it may seem that college and job interviews are a long way off, things you are doing online now may affect them strongly. Brenda Bench, author and career coach,

Students in Boston, Massachusetts, practice interview skills with business professionals. Thorough preparation for an interview, a carefully prepared résumé, and a positive online image are assets for a job applicant.

asked college and job recruiters what they found to be the worst mistakes applicants made in the interview process. The number one mistake, they agreed, was creating a negative Web image while in school or college. Bench found that, prior to the interview, almost half of recruiters researched an applicant's record online, using search engines such as Google. The applicant's entries on social networking sites like Facebook and LinkedIn were included in the searches.

It is important to think twice about what you post on blogs, personal Web sites, or social networking sites. When you are trying to impress or entertain your friends, it is all too easy to ruin your chances of entering the college or job you want, even before you apply or interview. Though the sites you join or visit may promise security and privacy, there is never any guarantee of that protection on the Web. No matter what you post online, it is always possible, even probable, that people you never intended or wanted to see it, will. This audience includes potential employers. Further, these negative posts can last forever. You can always change course, but you can rarely erase the tracks you have already made.

In turn, a good applicant will have used the Web to research a college or job before coming in for an interview. Interviewers notice if you have taken the time to learn about the college, organization, or business you are applying to. Also, your research will help you decide which aspects of your background you want to emphasize and which questions you want to ask the interviewer. Being well prepared to talk knowledgeably and enthusiastically about the college or job and to ask interesting questions will make a positive impression.

Don't Believe Everything You Read

As computer technology has increasingly become a central part of almost any career, good online research skills have become essential.

You may be a whiz at using your computer. You may know how your computer works and how to find information quickly. But if the information you retrieve in your research does not come from a reputable, qualified source, your paper or report may be judged unacceptable.

Arriving as a student on a college or tech campus that fits your needs is the reward for solid academic preparation and thorough research into post-high school opportunities.

When research was usually done from books in the library, students could be sure that most of the information they found was reliable. Editors carefully checked the facts before books were published, so researchers could depend on the information that they contained. Now, though, it is up to the student to investigate the sources of information that he or she finds on the Web before including the information in his or her paper or report.

Sometimes, the Web address or URL (e.g., http://www.pbs.org) gives enough information to judge whether the source is reliable, that is, whether the source carefully investigates information before publishing it. Other Web sites, however, may not be well-known sources. In that case, to be certain your report or paper contains correct information, you, the researcher, must verify the information by checking another source that you know to be reliable.

Wikipedia, for example, can be very useful in giving you an idea of what a subject is about. But since anyone can post information on Wikipedia without proving that he or she is qualified to write about the subject, most teachers won't accept Wikipedia as a valid source. Often an article gives references for the information it provides. Using those sources, when they are known to be reliable, can give assurance that the information is acceptable.

The Road to Success—in High School and After Graduation

Success is not a magic place where suddenly, someday, a guy will land if he is lucky. Success is finding yourself in the

WHAT WEB SITES CAN A GUY DEPEND ON?

There are a number of guidelines that you can follow to help determine whether a Web source is reliable. When you get the results of an Internet search, look carefully at the title, URL, and snippet of text provided by the Web browser. Good sites for research include:

- Web sites connected to a known university or college. URLs for these sites usually include ".edu."

- Web sites provided by government agencies. These URLs usually include ".gov."

- Web sites connected to reliable media news sources, such as known newspapers, magazines, TV channels, etc. The URLs usually include an abbreviation of the organization's name. Examples of well-known news sources include http://www.nytimes.com, http://www.cnn.com, http://www.abc.com, and http://www.npr.org.

- Web sites connected to nonprofit organizations, such as the United Nations, the American Cancer Society, or the American Red Cross. The URLs usually end in ".org." Verify these Web sites by reading the "About" section on the sites' home pages to learn more about the organizations.

place you intended to be because you planned, prepared, and took the necessary steps to get there. Your academic and career success will be made of a long series of day-to-day, year-to-year choices—often, tough choices—each made intentionally with your life goals in mind.

Along the way, you will need to avoid some traps. Some young men believe they should be tough enough to go it alone, and as a result, they never ask for help. These boys may needlessly find themselves in difficult school or career situations, ones that could have been avoided.

But tough choices don't have to be made alone. Take the initiative to accept or seek help whenever you need information, coaching, or guidance. Men and women who are farther along the road of life often feel honored when asked for their advice or specific help.

With you in the driver's seat, your life in high school, college, and beyond can be just what you decide to make it.

academic college A college that offers traditional scholarly courses.

ACT A national college admissions examination that consists of subject area tests in English, mathematics, reading, and science.

attention-deficit/hyperactivity disorder (ADHD) A behavioral disorder characterized by restlessness and the inability to focus attention for long periods of time.

blog A Web site, set up as a digital journal, in which users share thoughts, views, ideas, and images.

browser A computer program that locates Web sites or information.

deficient Not good enough; inadequate.

GED A test used to determine if a student has acquired skills and knowledge equivalent to earning a high school diploma.

globalization The development of an increasingly integrated global economy.

mentor A wise, trusted person who acts as a teacher or counselor to another person.

multilingual Able to speak, read, and understand more than one language.

peer pressure Social pressure by members of one's peer group to conform to the behaviors and wishes of the group.

proactive Tending to make decisions and take actions ahead of time, rather than reacting to events.

qualifications Special skills, abilities, experience, or knowledge that makes a person fit for a certain job or career.

résumé A written summary of a job or college applicant's work and academic experiences.

SAT A test used by colleges to determine how well an applicant is likely to perform at the college level.

shadow To accompany a person during the workday in order to learn about his or her job responsibilities.

technical college A college that offers courses that can lead to certification for various technical jobs and careers.

URL (uniform resource locator) The address of a specific Web site or file on the Internet.

Association for Career and Technical Education

1410 King Street

Alexandria, VA 22314

(800) 826-9972

Web site: http://www.acteonline.org

The Association for Career and Technical Education is a national education association dedicated to the advancement of education that prepares youth and adults for successful careers.

Boys & Girls Clubs of America

1275 Peachtree Street NE

Atlanta, GA 30309-3506

(404) 487-5700

Web site: http://www.bgca.org

The Boys & Girls Clubs help young people create aspirations for the future, providing opportunities for career exploration and educational enhancement. The organization aims to ensure that all club members graduate from high school on time, ready for a post-secondary education and a twenty-first-century career.

The Boys Initiative

Washington, DC 20001-5407

(888) 521-1745

Web site: http://www.theboysinitiative.org

The Boys Initiative is a groundbreaking national campaign to shed light on disturbing trends in recent years pertaining to boys' and young men's achievement. The organization's mission is to shed light on these issues, foster dialogue and debate about them, and collaborate on solutions.

Communities in Schools (CIS)

2345 Crystal Drive, Suite 801

Arlington, VA 2220

(703) 519-8999

Web site: http://www.communitiesinschools.org

CIS is a nationwide network of professionals working in public schools to
surround students with a community of support, empowering them to stay
in school and achieve in life. It is active in twenty-five states and the District
of Columbia.

Council of Ministers of Education, Canada (CMEC)

95 St. Clair Avenue West, Suite 1106

Toronto, ON M4V 1N6

Canada

(416) 962-8100

Web site: http://www.cmec.ca

Ministers of education work through the CMEC on a wide variety of activities,
projects, and initiatives related to education in Canada.

International Boys' Schools Coalition

700 Route 22

Pawling, NY 12564

(207) 841-7441

Web site: http://www.theibsc.org

The International Boys' Schools Coalition is a nonprofit coalition of schools from
around the world dedicated to the education and development of boys.

Say Yes to Education
320 Park Avenue, 20th Floor
New York, NY 10022
(212) 415-4590
Web site: http://www.sayyestoeducation.org/syte
Say Yes to Education is a national, nonprofit education foundation committed to
    dramatically increasing high school and college graduation rates for inner-city youth.

YMCA of the USA
101 North Wacker Drive
Chicago, IL 60606
(800) 872-9622
Web site: http://www.ymca.net
The YMCA offers programs to help underserved youth raise their academic standards,
    develop a positive sense of self, build character and leadership skills, explore
    diverse college and career options, and learn from role models and mentors.

Web Sites

Due to the changing nature of Internet links, Rosen
Publishing has developed an online list of Web sites
related to the subject of this book. This site is updated
regularly. Please use this link to access the list:

http://www.rosenlinks.com/ymg/21ed

Artis, Sharnnia. *Moving from Ordinary to Extraordinary: Strategies for Preparing for College and Scholarships.* New York, NY: iUniverse, 2008.

Chany, Kalman A., and Geoff Martz. *Paying for College Without Going Broke.* 2011 ed. New York, NY: Random House, 2010.

Christen, Carol, Richard Nelson Bolles, and Jean M. Blomquist. *What Color Is Your Parachute? For Teens: Discovering Yourself, Defining Your Future.* 2nd ed. Berkeley, CA: Ten Speed Press, 2010.

Davis, Sampson, George Jenkins, and Rameck Hunt. *The Pact: Three Young Men Make a Promise and Fulfill a Dream.* New York, NY: Riverhead Books, 2002.

Davis, Sampson, George Jenkins, and Rameck Hunt. *We Beat the Street: How a Friendship Pact Led to Success.* New York, NY: Dutton Children's Books, 2005.

Eastman, Linda. *The Young Man's Guide for Personal Success: For Teenage Boys and the People Who Love Them.* Prospect, KY: Professional Woman Publishing, 2008.

Ford, Marjorie. *The Changing World of Work* (Longman Topics). New York, NY: Pearson/Longman, 2006.

Gregory, Michael. *The Career Chronicles: An Insider's Guide to What Jobs Are Really Like: The Good, the Bad, and the Ugly from Over 750 Professionals.* Novato, CA: New World Library, 2008.

Lore, Nicholas, and Anthony Spadafore. *Now What? The Young Person's Guide to Choosing the Perfect Career.* New York, NY: Fireside, 2008.

MacDougall, Debra Angel, and Elisabeth Harney Sanders-Parks. *The 6 Reasons You'll Get the Job: What Employers Look for—Whether They Know It or Not.* New York, NY: Prentice Hall Press, 2010.

Pierce, Valerie, and Cheryl Rilly. *Countdown to College: 21 "To-Do" Lists for High School.* 2nd ed. Lansing, MI: Front Porch Press, 2009.

Roselius, J. Chris. *Surviving School: Managing School and Career Paths* (A Guy's Guide). Edina, MN: ABDO Publishing, 2011.

Silivanch, Annalise. *Making the Right College Choice: Technical, 2-Year, 4-Year* (Thinking About College). New York, NY: Rosen Publishing, 2010.

Tieger, Paul D., and Barbara Barron-Tieger. *Do What You Are.* 4th ed. Boston, MA: Little, Brown, 2007.

Unger, Harlow G. *But What If I Don't Want to Go to College? A Guide to Success Through Alternative Education.* 3rd ed. New York, NY: Checkmark Books, 2006.

U.S. Department of Labor. *Occupational Outlook Handbook, 2011–12 Edition.* New York, NY: Skyhorse Publishing, 2011.

Wolfinger, Anne. *Best Career and Education Web Sites: A Quick Guide to Online Job Search.* 5th ed. Indianapolis, IN: JIST Works, 2007.

American Museum of Natural History. "Hall of Human Origins." Retrieved February 15, 2011 (http://www.amnh.org/exhibitions/permanent/humanorigins/history/symbolic.php).

American Public Media: Marketplace. "Future-Jobs-O-Matic." Retrieved January 23, 2011 (http://marketplace.publicradio.org/features/future-jobs).

Australian Institute of Company Directors. "Directorship Matters: AICD Podcasts Interview with Prof. Howard Gardner: Boardroom Radio Webcast." October 10, 2007. Retrieved April 20, 2011 (http://www.brr.com.au/event/1ACD/60122/27697/wmp/e39dcpuj7c).

BBC News. "Infomania Worse Than Marijuana." April 22, 2005. Retrieved April 11, 2011 (http://newsvote.bbc.co.uk/mpapps/pagetools/print/news.bbc.co.uk/2/hi/uk_news/4471607.stm).

Benincasa, Robert. "Teenage Boys More Likely to Be in Fatal Car Crashes." NPR.org, November 25, 2009. Retrieved February 10, 2011 (http://www.npr.org/templates/story/story.php?storyId=120537839).

Blum, Deborah. Sex on the Brain: The Biological Differences Between Men and Women. New York, NY: Viking, 1997.

Boston.com. "In the Year 2016: The 30 Fastest-Growing Jobs." Retrieved March 6, 2011 (http://www.boston.com/jobs/galleries/30fastest_growing_occupations).

Brown, Robert M. "Dean's Message, Division of Continual Learning, UNCG." University of North Carolina–Greensboro, October 12, 2009. Retrieved January 21, 2011 (http://web.uncg.edu/dcl/web/about/about_dean.asp).

Carnevale, Anthony P., Nicole Smith, and Jeff Strohl. "Help Wanted: Projections of Jobs and Education Requirements Through 2018: Executive Summary." Center on Education and the Workforce, June 2010. Retrieved April 20, 2010 (http://cew.georgetown.edu/jobs2018).

Carson, Serenity. "The Importance of Learning a Foreign Language." November 5, 2008. Retrieved February 25, 2011 (http://www.associatedcontent.com/article/1162394/the_importance_of_learning_a_foreign.html?cat=4).

Centers for Disease Control and Prevention. "Injury Prevention & Control: Violence Prevention." October 2009. Retrieved June 2011 (http://www.cdc.gov/violenceprevention/pub/youth_suicide.html).

Centers for Disease Control and Prevention. "National Suicide Statistics at a Glance: Suicide Rates by Race/Ethnicity and Sex 10–24." September 30, 2009. Retrieved January 1, 2011 (http://www.cdc.gov/violenceprevention/suicide/statistics/rates03.html).

Centers for Disease Control and Prevention. "Surveillance Summaries." *Morbidity and Mortality Weekly Report*,

Vol. 55, June 9, 2006. Retrieved February 23, 2011 (http://www.cdc.gov/mmwr/PDF/SS/SS5505.pdf).

Chen, Su-Yen, and Yang-Chih Fu. "Internet Use and Academic Achievement: Gender Differences in Early Adolescence." *Adolescence*, Winter 2009. Retrieved February 19, 2011 (http://findarticles.com/p/ articles/mi_m2248/is_176_44/ai_n48846245/ pg_8/?tag=content;col1).

Goldstein, Arnold P. *Delinquents on Delinquency*. Champaign, IL: Research Press, 1990.

Graham, Erin. "The Teenage Brain." Dream Online, Children's Hospital Boston, 2008. Retrieved April 11, 2011 (http://www.childrenshospital.org/dream/ summer08/the_teenage_brain.html).

Greene, Jay P., and Marcus A. Winters. "Leaving Boys Behind: Public High School Graduation Rates." Manhattan Institute for Policy Research, Civic Report 48, April 2006. Retrieved February 23, 2011 (http:// www.manhattan-institute.org/html/cr_48.htm).

Kaiser Family Foundation. "Daily Media Use Among Children and Teens Up Dramatically from Five Years Ago." January 20, 2010. Retrieved January 16, 2011 (http://www.kff.org/entmedia/entmedia012010nr.cfm).

Kindlon, Daniel J., and Michael Thompson. *Raising Cain: Protecting the Emotional Life of Boys*. New York, NY: Ballantine Books, 1999.

Landy, Frank J., and Jeffrey M. Conte. *Work in the 21st Century: An Introduction to Industrial and Organizational Psychology.* 3rd ed. Malden, MA: Wiley-Blackwell, 2010.

Mayell, Hillary. "When Did 'Modern' Behavior Emerge in Humans?" *National Geographic News*, February 20, 2003. Retrieved January 20, 2011 (http://news. nationalgeographic.com/news/2003/02/0220_030220_humanorigins2.html).

McBride, Bill. "Boys Will Be Boys, Girls Will Be Girls: Teaching to Gender Differences." Retrieved February 17, 2011 (http://crr.math.arizona.edu/GenderKeynote.pdf).

National Aeronautics and Space Administration. "Astronaut Bio: Neil Armstrong." December 1993. Retrieved February 10, 2011 (http://www.jsc.nasa.gov/Bios/htmlbios/armstrong-na.html).

New Mexico Museum of Space History. "Inductee Profile: Yuri A. Gagarin." Retrieved February 10, 2011 (http://www.nmspacemuseum.org/halloffame/detail.php?id=8).

Olson, Lynn. "What Does 'Ready' Mean?" *Education Week*, June 12, 2007. Retrieved April 15, 2011 (http://www.edweek.org/ew/articles/2007/06/12/40overview.h26.html).

The Partnership for 21st Century Skills. "Life and Career Skills." 2004. Retrieved April 15, 2011 (http://www.

p21.org/index.php?option=com_content&task=view& id=266&Itemid=120).

Snyder, Howard N. "Juvenile Arrests 2005." *OJJDP Bulletin*, August 2008. Retrieved January 15, 2011 (http://www.ncjrs.gov/pdffiles1/ojjdp/218096.pdf).

The Three Doctors, Inc. "Our Story." 2007. Retrieved April 20, 2011 (http://www.threedoctors.com/ourstory.php).

University of Alabama Center for Teaching and Learning. "Causes of Failure in College." Retrieved April 9, 2011 (http://www.ctl.ua.edu/CTLStudyAids/StudySkillsFlyers/ GeneralTips/causesoffailure.htm).

U.S. Department of Health and Human Services. "What Challenges Are Boys Facing, and What Opportunities Exist to Address Those Challenges? Fact Sheet: Education." Retrieved April 15, 2011 (http://aspe. hhs.gov/hsp/08/boys/FactSheets/ed/index.shtml).

H

high-risk behavior and teen
  boys, 26
high school
  preparing for life after, 54–74
  succeeding in, 33–35, 38,
    39, 45, 46
humanitarian issues/needs, 18
Hunt, Rameck, 50–53

I

information
  explosion of, 11–13
  getting from Internet, 76–77
  obtaining basic, 32–38
information overload, 81
interest inventory test, taking a,
  57–58
Internet, 76–86
  getting information from,
    76–77, 84–86, 87
  mistakes made when using, 77,
    84–86
  negative Web image and,
    83–84
  time management and, 77–82
internships, 70
interviews, going on college or
  job, 72–74, 82–84

J

Jenkins, George, 50–53

K

knowledge
  doubling of over years,
    11–13
  obtaining basic, 32–38

L

language
  learning basic skills,
    33–35, 38
  reasons to learn a second, 16
laws, respecting, 43–46
learning in a changing world,
  13–17

M

masculinity, having to prove, 27
math, learning basic skills in, 33,
  35–38
mentor, getting a, 70

Q

questions to ask yourself about
  post–high school options,
  55–57

R

reading, importance of, 33–35
role models, 46–53
rules, respecting, 43–44

S

T

V

W

About the Author

Molly Jones writes on health and contemporary issues. She is the author of five previous books and several magazine articles and stories for children and young adults. She has a Ph.D. in educational research and additional graduate study in epidemiology and biostatistics. Her research has been published in *Medical Care, Remedial and Special Education,* and the *Journal of Early Intervention.* She lives on Lake Murray near Columbia, South Carolina.

Photo Credits